Malunda

Malunda

by **Louise Johnson**

pictures by **Edward DuRose**

Carolrhoda Books • Minneapolis, Minnesota

to my wonderful family, and to all those
striving to save endangered species like the
white rhino   —L.J.

to Aaron, Brian, Matt, and Tony   —E.D.

The author and publisher would like to express their appreciation to
the Whipsnade Park Zoo, Dunstable Beds, England, and especially to
V.J.A. Manton, Curator, for their help in the preparation of this book.

Publisher's Note: When animals like Malunda are captured, the crates
into which they are put are generally solid wood on all four sides and
open only at the top. However, in order to show Malunda inside it, an
open-sided crate has been depicted in the illustrations for this book.

8400086

Copyright © 1982 by Carolrhoda Books Inc.

All rights reserved. International copyright secured.
No part of this book may be reproduced in any form whatsoever
without permission in writing from the publisher except for
the inclusion of brief quotations in an acknowledged review.

Manufactured in the United States of America

LIBRARY OF CONGRESS CATALOGING IN PUBLICATION DATA

Johnson, Louise, 1916—
Malunda.

(A Carolrhoda on my own book)
Summary: A white rhinoceros and his herd are shipped
from Africa to a zoo in England, where the male becomes
angry and withdrawn, suffering from the loss of his horn
during capture.
1. White rhinoceros—Juvenile fiction. [1. White rhinoceros—Fiction. 2. Rhinoceros— Fiction] I. Durose, Edward,
ill. II. Title.

PZ10.3.J66Mal   [E]   81-15441
ISBN 0-87614-177-7   AACR2

1 2 3 4 5 6 7 8 9 10 87 86 85 84 83 82

NEW WORDS

Calves (kavz) Some animal babies are called calves.

Endangered species (in-DANE-jerd SPEE-sheez) A plant or an animal of which few are left in the world

Herd (herd) Some large animals, such as rhinos, travel in groups called herds.

Lioness (LIE-uh-nuhs) A female lion

Tranquilizer (TRANG-kwuh-LIE-zer) A drug used to put animals to sleep

Thick blue-gray skin
covered his body.
A long, pointed horn
curved back from his nose.
A second, shorter horn
sat right behind it.
A lioness watched him.
He charged a few feet toward her.
She hurried out of the way.
This animal was not afraid of lions.
He was a white rhinoceros.

This white rhino was still young.
But he was already 5 feet tall.
When he was full grown,
he would stand close to 6 feet tall.
He would be 14 feet long.
He would weigh about 4,000 pounds.
And his front horn
would grow to nearly 2 feet.
The young rhino was eating grass.
A small herd of white rhinos
was eating near him.
Most of them were females
or young calves.
Some day soon
he would be their leader.

A helicopter flew over the herd.

It made a lot of noise.

The young rhino started to charge.

But he could not find an enemy.

White rhinos are not usually fierce.

So he soon went back to eating.

Suddenly something stabbed him
in the shoulder.
The young rhino looked
from side to side.
He did not know what had hit him.
He started to run.

Other white rhinos were running
this way and that.
They had been shot
with tranquilizer darts.
The tranquilizer
would soon put them to sleep.
Men on horses followed the rhinos.
Soon the rhinos slowed down.
One by one they stopped.
Each one fell to the ground—asleep.
The riders used their radios to call
men who were waiting in trucks.
When the trucks got there,
the men put a rope
around each rhino's neck.

Then they gave shots to the rhinos
to make them wake up.
As the rhinos got to their feet,
the men used the ropes to lead them
into large wooden crates.
The men came
to the young male rhino last.
He had run farther than the others—
nearly a mile.
When they tried to lead him,
this rhino began to fight.
The men could see that
this wasn't going to be easy—
and it wasn't.

15

During the struggle,

the rhino's long horn broke off.

Only the short one was left.

But they finally got him

into the crate.

One man thought the male rhino

should have a name.

He called him Malunda.

Soon the others

called him Malunda too.

Malunda is an African name.

It means "the one with the big crest."

The white rhinoceros
lives in Africa.
It is an endangered species.
That means there are not many
of them left.
These men wanted to make sure
that there would always be
white rhinos.
They wanted the rhinos to have
plenty of food and water.
But mostly they wanted to protect
the rhinos from hunters.
So they were taking Malunda
and the others to a new home.

Inside the crate,

Malunda had enough room to stand up.

But there was not enough room

for him to turn around.

There was a bucket of water

in front of him.

There was also a pile of dried grass.

Malunda began to eat.

Soon all the crates
were loaded onto trucks.
The trucks took them to the sea.
It took all night.

When they finally got there,
a ship was waiting for them.
It would take the rhinos far away
to England.

A machine lifted Malunda's crate
high into the air.
The crate swung out over the ship.
Then it began to lower.
At last the crate was on the ship.
By now Malunda was acting strangely.
He was acting as if his head hurt.
As the boat began to move,
Malunda fell down on his side.

25

Several men stood in front
of Malunda's crate.
They could see he did not feel well.
They talked about his broken horn.
Men had fed and watered Malunda
since he had been put in the crate.
He did not seem to mind
having them near him.
One of the men was a doctor.
He talked to Malunda.
The doctor had a long-handled brush.
He put medicine on Malunda's nose
where the horn had been.

ENGLAND

27

Day after day,
the doctor put medicine
on Malunda's sore nose.
The doctor was worried.
The medicine was not helping.
Malunda had not eaten for days.
And he was much too warm.
He had a high fever.
"I'll have to give him a shot,"
the doctor told the men.
The doctor climbed on top
of Malunda's crate.
He reached down and pushed
a long needle into Malunda.
Malunda did not move.

"The wound is very bad,"
said the doctor.
"We will have to watch him
day and night."
The doctor and the men took turns.
They kept a close watch over Malunda.
They sprayed him with cold water.
They patted him and talked to him.
The ship sailed on toward England.

31

Many days passed.
Then one morning
Malunda began to eat his grass.
The man watching over him yelled.

"He's eating! Malunda's eating!"
The doctor came running.
He patted Malunda.
Malunda was cool again.

The men on the ship were happy.

They had become very fond of Malunda.

They liked to sit by his crate
during their time off.

For the rest of the trip,
Malunda ate very well.

The men gave him other foods
besides hay.

Malunda liked English muffins best!

By the time the ship got to England,
Malunda was fine.
He and the other white rhinos

were loaded onto trucks.
They were driven to the zoo.
At last the crates were unloaded.

Malunda was the first to be let out.

He dug his toes into the ground

and took a few steps.

The sun was shining.

Malunda blinked his eyes.

He turned around slowly.

The other rhinos were let out

to join Malunda.

They started to look for food.

White rhinos eat grass

and leafy plants.

These were growing all around.

There were ponds and streams too.

Malunda walked to a pond.
He lowered his head.
But he did not take a drink.
Instead, he acted as if
he was looking at himself
in the water.
He shook his head
and looked again and again.
He seemed ashamed
that his big horn was gone.

From that time on,
Malunda acted very strangely.
Even without his horn,
he was a beautiful white rhino.
But he stayed by himself
most of the time.
He kept away from the others
and ran around alone.
He acted angry.
Two years went by.
The men at the zoo were worried.
Rhinos have only one male leader
in each herd.
If Malunda kept on acting this way,
there would be no baby rhinos.

43

Then one day Malunda stood by a pond.
He could have seen himself
in the water.
The men watching him
were sure that he did.
They were sure he was looking
at his big new horn!
His horn was back again!
It wasn't quite as long
as it had been.
But it was pointed.
And it was beautiful!
Rhino horns are made
of hard clumps of hair.
So in time, they do grow back.

45

Malunda walked into the water.

He started to make

loud snorting noises.

He loped around.

He held his head high.

It looked as if

he was showing off that horn!

He pranced back and forth.

He snorted again,

as if he was telling the others

to come and join him.

They came running!

After that,

Malunda was calm and gentle again.

He stayed with the herd.

Soon it was clear that he would be
a great white rhinoceros leader.

ABOUT THIS STORY

Rhinoceroses have roamed the earth for 50 million years. And they haven't changed much in all that time. But today there aren't many rhinos left.

The white rhinoceros lives in Africa. Not long ago, white rhinos were nearly extinct (ehk-STINGKT). Extinct means that there are none left at all. But some people did not want that to happen. They started to capture small herds of white rhinos and move them to places where they would be safe. Because they are now protected, herds of white rhinos are getting larger.

MALUNDA is based on the true story of one white rhinoceros and his herd. In 1970, 20 white rhinos were captured in Africa and taken to the Whipsnade Park Zoo in England. The male rhino really was named Malunda, and his long horn really did break off during his capture. Malunda was treated on the ship and was well by the time the rhinos arrived at the zoo. But he acted very strangely. And he really did seem to look into the pond that day. But of course no one can know for sure if it was his reflection he was looking at.